Aimless Walk, Faithful River

Aimless Walk, Faithful River

Poems

by Simeon Dumdum Jr

bughaw

BUGHAW is an imprint of
ATENEO DE MANILA UNIVERSITY PRESS
Bellarmine Hall, Katipunan Avenue
Loyola Heights, Quezon City
P.O. Box 154, 1099 Manila, Philippines
Tel.: (632) 426-59-84 / Fax: (632) 426-59-09
E-mail: unipress@admu.edu.ph
Website: www.ateneopress.org

The National Library of the Philippines CIP Data

Recommended entry:

Aimless walk, faithful river : poems /
by Simeon Dumdum Jr. – Quezon City :
Ateneo de Manila University Press, 2017,
[c2017].
pages ; cm

ISBN 978-971-550-809-4

Bound with: The poet learns to dance (the dancer learns to write a poem)

1. Philippine poetry (English). I. Title.

899.2101 PR9550.6 2017 P720170254

Front cover artwork by Yana Durado
Book design by Adonis Durado

Contents

For Gingging

A Christmas Villanelle

I've known enough of joy to choose to stay
Through the Decembers when I could not find
Where grows the morning of a Christmas Day

Reasons there are, big ones, to go away
And there are pains that yearn to be defined
But I have known enough of joy to stay

A child had asked me at a time of play,
Perhaps a flower was what he had in mind,
"Where grows the morning of a Christmas Day?"

A flower snapped by bullets gone astray?
I asked myself, but it's another kind,
Of which I know a joy for which to stay

There was a birth, of a night faraway,
A word of light that had a world refined,
Where grows the morning of a Christmas Day

That world needs peace that does not know delay,
That offers, after leaving war behind,
Enough of joy for me to choose to stay
Where grows the morning of a Christmas Day

A Letter to Bob Dylan

Dear Bob, when "Blowin' in the Wind" came out
I was a secretive fourteen-year-old boy.
That same year, Sonny Liston scored a knockout
Against Floyd Patterson, and blind Ray Charles
Released his hit, "I Can't Stop Loving You."
Our lives allowed us only a few thrills,
We did have radio but no television.
In fact, three years would pass before I knew
Your song, and there was no comparison.

Are you a poet? Because there are those
Who label you as no more than a singer,
And since a singer does not dare compose
The lyrics purely for the page, he has
No place among the likes of Yeats and Eliot.
Bob, there are poems that seem to have class,
Which are bland dishes—the poems I'm seeking
Are those that taste of song, I want to bite
A real cheeseburger with everything.

A Lullaby for Francine

The infant in my arms
Eases to hear my voice
Intone a lullaby.
Just a week old, she stares
At me, but I don't know
If she sees me at all.
Still I gaze into her eyes
As though into a well,
On which my image floats.
I know, however, that
She listens to me singing,
Although I fear that she
Could not make head or tail
Of it, for what is it,
This *too-la-roo-ra-li,*
But a caress that's hummed,
And what is a caress
Except a lullaby
Embedded in embrace,
Which every infant needs
To sleep.

A Note to Myself, to Be Read upon Reaching Old Age

Knowing the trip could last an hour,
I brought along Szymborska's *Map*,
A book I could dip into when
The view or traffic asked for it.
Mother-in-law, who's 92,
Sat in the backseat with the aide,
Not quietly by any means,
Because she kept on asking questions,
Which with respect and kindness we
Answered again and yet again.
We reached a section of the city
Surrounded by shop signs and billboards,
Which she read, each of them, aloud.
I should have looked at what she read,
But did not—now I realize
That I was being snobbish, for,
While I was just reading a book,
She really was reading the world.

A Rose for St. Therese

Therese, each time I see a rose
I think of you—why, I don't know,
Although there was a time you said
You would let fall a shower of roses.
I could imagine a bright morning
When suddenly the sky pours down
Roses, Old Roses—Lady Banks,
Baronne Prevost, Francis Dubreuil,
And others, mostly with French names—
Not to forget the Hybrid Teas—
Double Delight, Elina, Peace.
Chrysler Imperial, and the like—
The petals drifting not so much
On the air as on the light,
And we would live our lives under
The splendor of a great Rose Window.
The world's most beautiful rose gardens
Must look with envy at the sky.
What roses did you mean, Therese,
And why already do I see them
Falling like feathers to the ground?
I could catch one of them at will
And hold its stem towards the light,
Rose, less of window than of wonder.

Afternoon

What's with the afternoon? After a nap,
I thought I had begun to understand
The link of sleep to luminosity,
How always one would give way to the other,
Reversible both like a palindrome,
Because it was bright noon when I lay down
And dreamt of roaming a field of gardenias
That seemed so real I woke up half-expecting
To find myself enveloped with their fragrance.
But there was none, there was only the breeze
Moving the window curtains back and forth,
The light entering the gap between them,
Pulsing like a butterfly on the sofa.

Aimless Walk, Faithful River

Our exchange kept us deaf
To our steps' conversation,
Blind to where we were going.
At times the tall grass flashed
The quail's abrupt leap from
Our feet, and we fell silent,
Wondering how fear had
Propelled a small bird skywards
To find a hiding place
Beyond sight, having traced
A rainbow into freedom,
And then the words came back,
More seen this time than heard
Because they now described
The landscape—yellow bells,
Cadena de amor,
The little pink cups clustered
Against the sudden gusts,
Jade vines above the stream,
Turquoise flowers, butterflies
With flight deferred, their wings
Folded—the distance held
Its measure from the light
As we kept to the path
That flowed like a stroke of writing
Across a field of weeds,
Scripting the afternoon,
And which the river read
Again and again and again.

Being a Nocturne, Which Is a Starry Story

Outside was cool and without hint of rain.
I thought of being alone in the open.
And watching stars? But that's another story,
You are the weather on which all depends.

I thought of being alone in the open.
Out in the windy silence there were fireflies.
You are the weather on which all depends,
The cloud of light that quickly disappears.

Out in the windy silence there were fireflies
I wish I could commingle with your hair,
The cloud of light that quickly disappears
At the wave, the slightest wave of a hand.

I wish I could commingle with your hair
The night itself, which was out there with me,
At the wave, the slightest wave of the hand,
It would have claimed my coming and my going.

The night itself, which was out there with me,
From where in the air there was scent of jasmine,
It would have claimed my coming and my going
Had I not heard the echo of my name.

From where in the air there was scent of jasmine
I came inside because you called for me.
Had I not heard the echo of my name
I could have gone out to the porch to smoke.

I came inside because you called for me.
Outside was cool and without hint of rain.
I could have gone out to the porch to smoke

Christ Risen by Rubens

Neither this, by Peter Paul Rubens,
Nor any of the other paintings,
Could show us the first thing about
The Resurrection of the Christ.
Nobody saw it happening.
The gardener might have descried
Something extraordinary,
If he did not turn out to be
Jesus himself, whom Magdalene
Mistook for keeper of the garden,
Whose flower buds next to the tomb
Must have unfolded in the night
To watch a twist in history,
And if I were investigating
I'd find each craning lily stunned
Like the eye stabbed by a sharp light.
Rubens interprets what the flowers,
Their gaze transfixed by what they saw,
Witnessed, all of which must have occurred
At the same time that the big rock
Flipped over and then rolled away
From the cave's mouth—Rubens shows us
Jesus about to rise just as
A red-robed angel lifts the shroud
From him, while on the left two cherubs
Poise a looped crown upon his head—
Odd that in this painting Christ has
A sensuous and worldly body
With just a vague trace of his wounds,
Unlike the Christ in Rembrandt's version,
Who intermingles with the brightness,
Which might be closer to the truth—
The eyes of man as well as flowers
Are boggled by excessive light,

Which God's unveiling ever is,
But this is Rubens after all,
Who painted such as the *Three Graces*,
In which he fetes the human form,
Which lies in a balance between
Shapeliness and deformity,
Whole and frail like gossamer.
If anything, Christ made the body
More beautiful by his rising.
No other body was more tattered
Than his own, none other more ugly
Than the dead, but he rose to life
With the strength and beauty that Rubens
Could impart using his paintbrush,
With more, in fact, infinitely more.
Still, for us Rubens is a start,
Because we cannot ask the lilies,
The irises and asphodels,
That chose to bloom on Easter morning.

Cynghanedd

A rose appears at a veranda,
Respires at every node
Of slender, rain-washed leaf,
A vessel under no wish to loaf,
Despite the joyful hours.
Days pat the edgy flowers.

What words do I have now?
A white way ride, said a heaven.
A mouth spews out light.
Moths pass a tale out
Of sigh candles in silence,
A voice canoe idles on icy lanes.

Listen, I need to hold you
Less now in doubt how old.
Windows small as birds,
Owned as smiles, as brides,
Open to morning
Upon a time running.

Dear Basho

Dear Basho, what's this?
A frog jumps into a pond
Shattering the full moon!

Geography Lesson

The most effective teacher is our terror.
Kalashnikovs make the best pointing sticks,
And, thanks to them, our grasp of politics
And geography has grown with the hour.
Children, spread out the map now on the counter
And find Kabul and Nice, where lunatics
Massacred innocent people—the graphics
You should omit, I have to give that order.
Geography as a subject is tough,
Unlike before when it was a bright doorway
To a world sunned by beauty—that's all, chaps,
You look so troubled, you have had enough
Of good, old world geography today.
Until tomorrow, or next week perhaps.

How Their Heirs Turn Tyrants into Heroes

Because, like all of us, the tyrants die,
The first thing their heirs do is make us all
Forget, so that we will not long forestall
Their burial among heroes, then they lie,
They use their loot and backers to deny
The real facts behind their parents' fall,
Make their lives charm us instead of appall,
And turn them into symbols to live by.

And we, due to the smallness of our lives,
Because we need to last when day is gone
To keep the home and children out of danger,
Live with their lies, until the time arrives
When we forget, when this we should have done—
Remember and remember and remember.

Jared and Julia

When Julia, eight months old,
Cries for her morning milk,
Jared, her little brother,
Runs for the baby bottle
Their mother has prepared,
And puts the rubber nipple
In Julia's waiting mouth,
And in this demonstration
Of inborn human love
I hear the wind and rain
Stirring the buds awake,
And the birds chirping from trees
Yearning for sustenance
From thoughts of home
Now left as far behind
As the bright, crumbling stars.
The clock ticks with the soft
Pulsing of Julia's throat.
I see two tendrils rising,
One holding up the other,
To the enlarging yellow
Of the clear, growing hours.
I smile at our grandchildren,
One bailing out the other
So early on life's sea
With its exigencies
That seek the sudden harbor
Of the beloved's arms.
As Jared holds the bottle
With his small steady hand
And Julia at the teat
Quaffing the clement milk,
Her hand grasps Jared's thumb—
I see a little bird
Clutching the tiny branch
While feeding on its flower.

Lai for Daughter Genevieve on Her Birthday

Since today's your day
What is there to say
But this
May time not delay
Nor burdens outweigh
Your bliss

And as the day grows
And draws to a close
Tell me
The tale you propose
The vision that shows
The sea

May love be as wide
And God be implied
In dreams
May tomorrow's tide
Bear joys alongside
As themes

Leafing Through a Love Story

Little leaves emerge as you bask in sunlight.
I could never miss them, the book in my hands
Notwithstanding, reading across the garden always with raised eyes.

Leaves or tendrils, tenderly curling eastwards,
Showing where the labyrinth's center holds you,
Thread the story, linking it page by page, to end up in your arms.

Looking for Mt. Fuji

It rained—the Tokyo Metropolitan
Government Building darkened for a while,
Veiling the presence of a fitful spring
That shed its shyness with a burst of sun
As we approached a side street in Shinjuku.
We had to ask whoever came around
To show us where to go, travel had made us
Beggars in Tokyo, beggars for directions,
Stopping three young ladies in black with questions,
And they surrounded us, all set to help,
Except that they misheard what we were saying
And with regret denied knowing the building,
Which was in fact just right in front of us—
Language may hide what is closest, just as
The meteorological may obscure it.
Case in point, Mt. Fuji in central Honshu,
All sixty miles southwest of Tokyo, which,
The brochures said, we could see from the building.
And yet, when we got to the viewing site,
Floor 45, Mt. Fuji was invisible,
A haze had covered where they said it was.
But I was not deterred, after an hour
I hied back to the window, this time lucky
To find that a mountain towards the left
Of the snow-capped Fuji was clear of clouds,
Its rising slope the start of a handwritten
Message, whose most important word, however,
A drop of rain had smudged, as though Mt. Fuji
Were a code, kept secret by time, by weather.

Mactan Channel

Loathe to disappear before night the bright sea.
As we watch, the afternoon starts to fall back.
Boats begin their voyage for home across the channel, moving without sound,

Leaving you and me in the grudging last light.
We converse again in a void without words,
And although the darkness engulfs the land, it fails to dim your sun.

In the dusk I still could discern the blue strip
That the boats have taken to hide and be safe,
And we head for home by the sea, which is the last thing to get dark

Monsoon

That it should end up on this very landing
Is not a wonder, different things unravel
On this porch, more so with the weather changing—
Leaves, of course, on the last leg of their travel,
A dying moth about to lose the battle,
And now, a paper plane, far from the storms
Of a boy's sobbing in his mother's arms.

Nice, France

She could have sent a postcard, a photograph
Of Le Negresco, Nice's high-end hotel,
Proof that she and her husband were really there,
Posing in front of the building that stands by the Promenade des Anglais, and I would have let out a laugh,
Delighted that our friends had travelled to Côte d'Azur,
In Nice, playground of many a restless royal
And rootless artist, enamored of its sea as well as its light, which moved Matisse to declare
How tender it was and how gentle.
But somehow something vile
Happens, stopping a deed so innocuous
As witnessing to or portraying the beautiful,
And suddenly we saw Le Negresco turn into a center to house
The dying and wounded for a brief, chancy while.

How I wish there were someone to save them,
Not the cops, who were helpless to halt the scum,
An artist perhaps, if art's light had more fire and were more truly light, a Chagall of prayer,
Whose brush made its subjects defy falling,
And that night, on the Promenade des Anglais,
After the fireworks, before the lorry forced its way
Into the crowd, it could have lifted the people into the air
And sent the men, women, and children joyfully flying.

Nothing Is Heard Except What Is Remembered

I know this was the place that we deserted:
A room, a garden—dahlias in a vase?
But nothing comes to mind except the flowers,
Perhaps a letter, too, nothing is certain.

A room, a garden—dahlias in a vase?
Birds fly to write a note across the window,
Perhaps a letter, too, nothing is certain
But images that shift at every moment.

Birds fly to write a note across the window,
A mirror of goodbyes and silences,
The images that shift at every moment,
The constant, random shuffling of the cards.

A mirror of goodbyes and silences,
The falling leaves, the echoes of themselves,
The constant, random shuffling of the cards,
Shadows that leave the hands and then return.

The falling leaves, the echoes of themselves,
Of words that are repeated, and the gestures,
Shadows that leave the hands and then return,
While on your breast I press an ear to sleep.

Of words that are repeated, and the gestures,
There's little that I can remember now.
While on your breast I press an ear to sleep,
I try recalling what was left behind.

There's little that I can remember now.
I know this was the place that we deserted.
I try recalling what was left behind,
But nothing comes to mind, except the flowers.

November

Dear November, come within view of our hope.
Rain has veiled our eyes, but the hour is near dawn.
No October moon can stay up to cut our craving for sunrise.

So we wait, because in the morning things change.
Fears do not survive the ingress of pure light.
Laughter breaks up darkness the way the thought of light parts the sad night.

Ode to Butter Shaped Like a Rose

Yellow rose, how wonderful meeting you here.
Seeing you so small and delightful, can I
Ever eat you casually, breakfast being mainly of salt bread?

Roses are my thing, and jasmine, and you too,
Now that you have taken the form of butter
On a small dish, silently blooming, petals still wet with dewdrops.

Then you quickly disappear, like a real flower.
Much as I would like to defer the feeding,
Human as I am, I would have to violate your frail rosehood.

I confess that I hesitate to do this.
Contemplation, nonetheless, has its clear bounds.
So I scoop you up with a little prayer, and thanks, for our brief lives.

Ode to the Last and Smallest Tomato on the Table

So you escaped the knife
Or perhaps it escaped you
Because you are too small,
Or red, evoking sunset,
Whose sky no lightning knifes
Until it turns dark gray
(As yet the weather owes
The world no violence).

Being the last tomato
Means that you've been ignored,
Too small to be of use
Except to call up silence,
Or prompt indifference,
Perhaps because assassins
Will waste no bullet on
The tiniest of tomatoes,
Or wield a knife on something
That merely looks like blood
That dripped down from its point,
Red globule on the ground,
One of the many spilled
With every quick knife thrust
Or sudden burst of gun.

What happens on the streets
Should not happen to you—
No gun or knife should come
To hurt the last and smallest
Tomato on the table.

On Beauty

He seemed a paragon of health and wholeness,
Although I heard that he had a disease,
Which made me think after our casual meeting
If indeed healing is but the rebuilding
Of parts to their original condition,
And as for that, is beauty completeness
And so depends on what is physical?
Of course, my memory of a beautiful thing,
Such as a rose, I gain from actual roses
That I have seen and touched and smelled, and then
I get the notion of a perfect rose,
Which is not physical and has no parts—
These questions have haunted me since we met,
Because his handshake was firm and complete,
Although, when I was shaking his right hand,
I noticed that it had two fingers missing.

On Seeing a Photograph of Sawi

He stands beside a door
Older than he, behind him
Shadows, older still

Prayer for Rodrigo Duterte

Lord, we present to you this man, Rodrigo.
No one has walked the land quite like this Django,
This native cowboy who believes in Jesus,
I think, because his mouth is full of curses,
Although there might be more honesty there
Than on respectful lips full of hot air.
But, Lord, the Holy Gospels do impart
That the mouth speaks from the wealth of the heart,
But who can judge this except yourself, Lord,
Your ears, all-hearing, record every word
And measure it against that yardstick, truth.
Still, Lord, Rodrigo's language is uncouth,
And if you find my unease evident
It is because he is our President.

Lord, he's a man who thinks little of killing
(That was what he said when he was campaigning.)
Of course, he meant slaying the criminals,
Above all, those who disregard the signals
For them to stop—but Lord all life belongs
To you, who heal and rectify all wrongs.
But people cannot wait, they are impatient,
And the police and courts are inefficient.
So hang the law, we all want to be safe.
Are we, each of us, really that naif?

The sinner, said the French poet Charles Péguy,
Is at the heart of Christianity.
I admit, Lord, that we have all done wrong.
Even the saints, they sing a sinner's song,
But deeper, wider, higher than all this,
God's mercy waits for us, the Father's kiss.
The Book of Lamentations keeps reminding—
God's love's not spent, is renewed every morning.
Forgive him, Lord, if he did what he said,
Forgive us, Lord, the ill thoughts in our head.

Lord, bless and guide our leader from the south.
His heart's in the right place? But not his mouth,
Which last he said was just for politics,
His cursing and tough stance no more than antics.
Still his compassion has spawned many stories.
Who is he really, why the endless queries?

Of course, you know Rodrigo, Lord, the same
That as a boy was sent to call your name
And ask forgiveness by a concerned mother,
Nanay Soling, after a misdemeanor,
And this was when he faced the Crucified,
And, in his boyish innocence, he tried
To assure Jesus of his company
As he performed the imposed penalty—
Kneeling before him who was sacrificed,
His arms outstretched as were the arms of Christ.

Questions Asked at a Writers' Workshop After Sawi Said That He Held a Dog Before a Mirror

The dog barked.
Why?
Was it because Sawi carried it?
Was it because it wanted to be put down?
Did it at that moment think of something
worth barking at?
(When dogs think, aside from barking,
they point up their ears.)
Did anything run in the room, which
it wanted to chase?
Or was it because it saw itself in the mirror?
If so, which barked first, the dog outside
or the dog inside the mirror?
Or perhaps it was because, when the dog
saw itself in the mirror, in Sawi's arms,
its joy was doubled.

Rain and Memory

How do I want to be remembered, now
That it's about to rain, but does it matter?
As I breathe into the garden, the weather
Changes, the flowers, though they always bow,
Do not have memory, no matter how
Warm the touch of sun or loud the patter
Of rain, and nothing that is here will ever
See me intently gazing out the window.
Except a small child passing by, a tyke,
Whom a dog follows, his pet, and for a brief
Moment, a moment without hesitation,
They look at me with eyes that seem like
Four raindrops falling on a taro leaf,
And rolling down, carrying my reflection.

Shinjuku

An ancient pond
A frog jumps in
The sound of water
— Basho

Because, when he wrote it, he was in Edo,
The name of Tokyo in the poet's time,
I might be looking at the same old pond
That Basho viewed, or something similar,
At the traditional Japanese garden
There in Shinjuku Gyoen, which had drawn us
That April month to watch the cherry blossoms.
What Basho contemplated was the moment—
Tick of a frog's jump and tock of its splash,
The swinging of the pendulum as toad—
And I took it that, like me Basho stood
Under a canopy of cherry blossoms
While glancing at the water, which my wife
Included in the photographs she took
Of me, reminding me of prohibitions,
Because I was about to throw a stone
Into the pond in Basho's memory.
Neither could I pick any of the blossoms
That in their light pink fragility hung
Above, a reminder of beauty's passing
In the rain of flowers at the slightest wind,
But not without a chance for me to smile,
Because there was a sudden fall of petals,
And what the state refused to give to us
The breeze so kindly laid on my wife's hair.

Sijo

So tired of walking, with the hours always a step ahead,
You kick whatever gets in the way, including the peonies,
But not the shadows, which always find something to hide behind.

And, even when you rest, there are footsteps, the roll of dead leaves.
Lie down and cover your face with a fedora and sleep,
Until someone lifts the hat, a passerby rude as the wind.

How far do you have to go, since fields recede as you approach,
And you never get to ride the horse that no one sends you,
Or which, because you left no one behind, cannot find you?

Friend, if the rainy night flashes its knives, face it alone,
But if your old heart is not up to it, just run for cover,
Which may be in her arms, if she meets you, if only you love her.

Friend, rise up and count the stones that line the road between you and her.
It may be that you will lose count if you find that the door is closed.
Go back over with the memory and count the stones again.

Sometimes It Is Not Good to Stand While Singing

They stood in front of us, all five of them,
Blind eyes with shades—the second veil of darkness.
They started strumming their guitars and sang
Of love—of a young girl singing of love,
Which was for them and her a double light,
For her song was the song of her own people—
Tikadong, tikadong, tikadong, tikadong, tikadong—
Which we all sang, the blind and the not blind,
Everyone singing, seated, except one—
I found myself standing in front of them
And was embarrassed by my uselessness:
I seemed to have no role, except that of
Conductor of a band of blind musicians.

Song as Mirror of Morning

Morning splits into gardens
Gardens give way to dahlias
Dahlias evoke your arms
Your arms augur bright weather
Bright weather sets off brown warblers
Brown warblers emit soft calls
Soft calls inhabit blessings
Blessings preoccupy hands
Hands measure the sea
The sea importunes the land
The land forgets the sea
The sea keeps changing hands
Hands touch off blessings
Blessings suspire with soft calls
Soft calls release brown warblers
Brown warblers criss-cross bright weather
Bright weather becomes your arms
Your arms confide in dahlias
Dahlias ride with the gardens
Gardens slide into morning

Song of the Dead

Should it be heavenly?
But that would trivialize
The manner of their death—
From a black loneliness
With neither door nor window,
From the bone-ripping pain
Of a relentless cancer,
From a blast after the cold feel
Of a gun on the temple,
A glimpse of a masked face.
And yet they have a song.
They died with open mouths
As though about to sing it,
And not be silenced
By silence.

Street Scene

Each time I see a bundle on the street,
Wrapped in tarpaulin, a blanket or newspaper,
I get a lump in my throat—it's as if
Someone has handed me a telegram
(Many a time the bearer of bad news).
But then that wild horse, the imagination,
Can become too wild for its rider, reason,
Which needs to rein it in with arguments,
Such as that things like blankets and tarpaulins
Will likely end up on the city streets
As much as plates and cups, the first to fly
Outside the door in a domestic spat,
And if too neat to be the crop of chaos,
A passerby has tucked the bundle in,
Unable to resist a tidy fit.
As to newspapers, they're there all the time,
And the wind strangely has a way of forming
The front and inside pages into figures,
Even into the likeness of a corpse
(I call that the revenge of history).
At times, I see shoes stick out of the bundle.
Again, I tell myself, the streets accept
All sorts of rubbish, even underwear,
And who knows if someone's feet had outgrown
The shoes, or somehow he had lost his feet,
Or, God forbid, his life—and I just hope
They did not throw his body into the street
Together with his shoes.

Summer Solstice

The birds that reach the harbor
Never fly back to sea.
They ditch the sky in circles.
Bicycles that roam the quay
Pass by a tree
Where birds have come for shelter.

I gaze at one of them
On a stem holding up
A scented little flower,
Our choice of a dew cup
That's worth a trip,
Brief beauty's algorithm.

The orange-breasted sunbird
Has stirred, and I refuse
To come much closer, knowing
Something of this recluse—
That it would choose
To leave is not absurd.

But it won't lose its shelter,
Ever a true concern,
Not on a summer solstice.
Notice how the hours yearn
To return
To the tree by the harbor.

Sunrise in Owak

We wanted to surprise the sea,
Still the sea managed to surprise us.
We got up early, at sunrise,
But the sun failed to flower through
A growth of clouds towards the east,
Which the sea tried to compensate
With a light mirrored from nowhere.
To have the sea for ourselves was
What we had hoped for, but already
There were boats being paddled home,
Women and children pulling up
The still submerged net from the deep,
Their movements were all that we noticed,
A slow dance to the waves' whispers,
The lowest on the scale of sound.
A dog sat on the water's edge
Facing the ocean, but the boats
Had arrived, there was nothing else
But time, the turning of the tide.
Perhaps it waited for a presence,
Which might be in another sea,
A wider, deeper sea within us.

Supermoon

So which moon is it
The one above the trees or
The one in your eyes

The All-Embracing Shade of Smallness

That tree, it is now fully grown,
Sturdy and prodigal of shade,
And yet, not seven years ago,
It was no more than a thin sapling.
The cab I took had stalled before it
And I could find no covering
From the enraged midmorning sun
Except its leaves, which were not much,
And could no more stop the sunlight
Than a sieve could the falling water,
But which did not prevent its branches,
Small as they were, from giving me
Whatever little shade they could,
Persisting to do this as though
What really mattered was their presence.
And I recalled a little girl,
My daughter, almost three years old,
Who, when I acted being scared,
Quickly approached to hold my hand
And assure me of her protection.

The Falling Man

A magazine called him "The Falling Man,"
The one who jumped or dropped from the North Tower
That dreadful day, eleventh of September,
Photographed falling as the fire began
To burn the tower down, and people ran
Or leapt to bolt its flames—the lens' capture
Of the poor man is perfect, which will ever
Be in our minds, banish it if we can.
The image shows the man still in the air
And him no time or gravity can seize.
I see him as a feather that God blesses
With His gentle breath that is everywhere.
Yet what this photograph does is just freeze
The moment—but the moment freezes us.

The Light Inside the Room Within Me

So when I push the door, the light goes in
Ahead of me, a true and faithful dog,
As though to nose a quarry and unclog
The room of darkness, for me to begin
To see, and clear my doubts, and be forgiven.
The light becomes me as I catalogue
The things I have, and check the analog
Clock for the time, and set the time within.

Augustine said that the mind needs a light
Outside itself as pair, like man and wife,
To know the truth, attain clarity,
And certainly I have to set things right,
Enter an inner room, and choose a life
That's lived in the light of eternity.

The Light of Truth, the Truth of Light

Tell me if something's not right with my eyes,
Because you think that I am squinting, but
It's just a ploy, I really want to cut
The view to what I feel should be its size.
If I may say so, this is an exercise
I do each time I fall into a rut,
When everything I see has undercut
The truth, of which I get only a slice.

Say if nothing else is available.
Because the more the shelves, the less the freedom,
Which contemplates—more than just gathering
The goods—the embrace of the invisible,
Why I close my eyes, and not open them,
Because in darkness light is everything.

The Mind's a Palimpsest of Sea and Memory

Far may I canter from my country.
No art is an inn on routes unknown.
One raring to douse in roaring tides
Listens to shovels lose no stash of lies.
As a phone expires, a phoenix appears
From nowhere, a fiery aim in a whirr
Of silence, a vessel on a sea
Subtly vain, so still even as
An ocean rolls an ashen release
Into sunset, night's nest.
No art but memory, one hour to ebb time, your
Arms remember a room's raw ember.

The Old Man and the Sea

After his dog died, he now walks alone
Along the shore, hoping still that his precious
Companion would return. A bad calf bone
Slows him down, but no rush—he presupposes
That one wave surging, reaching the shore as
A ripple lapping his feet with devotion,
Is as yet just days away in the ocean.

The Photograph as Profile of Our Pain

This odd, disturbing photograph concerns
A five-year-old boy, his head dyed with blood,
Seated in a chair in absolute silence.
He might as well be the fossil of one
On whom volcanic dust had settled, drifting
For years—this photograph begs our compassion

Because the heart's a river of compassion
If not curved in upon its own concerns.
The sight of you, Omran, arrests its drifting,
Turns it into a rage pulsing with blood
To stop what seeks to kill the helpless one,
A force that enfleshes the bones of silence.

In Syria, the night had sunk into silence
When the bombs came, falling without compassion,
And of your little family no one
Was spared, the desert sky had no concerns
Other than violence, the flow of blood,
The people running, crying, or just drifting.

Omran, you sat there as though you were drifting
In a sad amniotic sac of silence,
Hair tousled and covered with dust, the blood
About to cake, awaiting our compassion,
As we await the birth of our concerns
For life, for death, for which we strive as one.

In Aleppo, bombs that fell one by one
Sent the burst bodies of the people drifting
On a current of fire, there were concerns
That there was life still buried in the silence
And there you were, midwifed by our compassion,
Delivered from the debris still with blood.

The war is as old as yourself, the blood
That stained your head you tried to wipe with one
Stroke of the hand, and this caught our compassion
Off guard, its innocence sending us drifting
From sympathy to anger and to silence,
And guilt, at the smallness of our concerns.

For what concerns us is not just the blood
But your stare and your silence, that of one
Drifting beyond the reach of our compassion.

The Voyage Leads to an Abandoned Heart

Electrodes on my every leg and arm,
As well as, glued with cold gel, on my chest,
I lay, the boat of my body at rest,
Moored to the machine, and somehow I felt warm,
As though a thermal air had risen from
A sea under my bed, but it was just
My thoughts (and I blamed it on my headrest),
And then it stopped, the boat had left the storm.
The nurse told me the ECG had ended,
Tore off from the machine part of the chart,
On which was written, as though on a bandage,
An undecipherable word, repeated
Over and over, as if my poor heart
Were in distress, and sending me a message.

The Wood of Sacrifice

The typhoon took their homes
And lives away—the waves
Ripped the outriggers off
And smashed the fishing boats
Against the rocks—the winds
Coiled themselves around
The fragile wooden houses,
Which escaped being pulled up
By bending, bowing, kneeling,
And breaking up to flounder
In the rain's spinning chalice.
The angry waters forced
A homeless fisherman
To hang on to a tree.

The people stored the rubble
In a pile—broken oars,
Fractured posts, shredded walls,
Those no one had use for,
At the back somewhere, all
But irretrievable,
Until a stranger with
Far out ideas came
And asked for wood, the bits
Of boats, the pieces of
The posts and walls, and even
The tree where someone died,
And then put them together,
Chiseled them, sawed and hammered,
And when the man had finished
The people saw an altar.
The lives of those who died
The folk could not retrieve,
But through the odds and ends
Of what remained of them

Was formed a table for
What they had sacrificed.
They knew that if there was
A dying on the altar
There also was a rising.

Time and Rodrigo Duterte

Of course, if you hate him,
Nothing he does will merit
Your thumbs-up, no, not even
When he looks at his watch,
As in this photograph
Of him sitting before
A table of Coke cans.
Why should he check his watch?
Why should he be like us,
Worried about appointments
And then fly into cursing
When time outpaces us?
But for Rodrigo Duterte
There is no time to kill.
Time is a fugitive,
But not a criminal,
Who, like Schrödinger's cat,
At once both lives and dies.
The moments must arrive
Whatever the consensus.
How truly undemocratic
Are the clock's hands, which never
Go up for a viva voce.
A dramatist who laughed
At Time, George Bernard Shaw,
Said that, like cobras loose
In a playground or garden,
Whose necks we break forthwith
Without trial by jury,
The criminal who cannot
Be reformed must be killed
As a necessity.
But has Rodrigo read
Shaw and found him apropos?
And when he checks his watch

Is it to verify
If once again there is
Another human gnomon
Falling to join his shadow?
Or is it just to check,
Like any other father,
If it is time for Kitty,
His daughter, to be home.

Where I Am, Everything Speaks of Nothing but You

Where I am, everything speaks of nothing but you
Being the season, the windblown leaves' turning,
Which precedes all ripeness and calls on daylight
To approach on tiptoe because rains veil your sleep.

Your voice has borne silence as a vase the lily
That blooms with pure posture always,
And I would pick it up, if you speak and your words become petals,
Sprouting from the last tips of your shy white light.

And if you walk by, your shadow across
The path will spawn everything that I have never been,
And no desire will return without wisdom.
With such yearning will I search for your laughter.

What I know is that, with you here, no one else offers
The perfume of your form, whose lithe swaying pours around me
The unseen and slow river of easy jasmine,
All that remains after everything disappears.

It may be that beauty, as we know it, is passing.
Your arms have broken loose from the hours' insistence,
Leaving with a wave the lessons gained from falling,
Which I must relearn alone if you walk away.

New Journalism

Rain fell after the newsboy came
And left the morning paper lying
On the front yard, as he does always.
We were then sleeping when the drops
Hit doors and windows like blind insects,
Exploding, leaving wings of water
Splattered about the yard and patio.
But they had stopped when I awoke
And all I saw was just the wreckage
Collecting into little puddles,
And then I saw the soaked newspaper,
Still of a piece under a film of water,
The sadness of the woman in
The photograph on the front page
Intact, as was her story, which
Continued on page twenty five,
Beside reports of robberies,
Falling economies and wars.
I tried to lift the pages up,
But, as I did, the paper crumbled,
The sogginess lopped off the headline
From the main body of the news,
Which soon became no more than fragments,
And piece by piece I tried to put
Together what remained—mine was
A new form of news gathering.

In the tradition of the great Romantic poets,
Simeon Dumdum Jr.'s *Aimless Walk, Faithful River*
is a delicious meandering through lush poetic landscapes in a relentless search for those wellsprings that make us fully human and fully alive.
Blending his superb lyrical and narrative gifts
with an effortless mastery of poetic forms,
Dumdum meditates on the consolations of nature,
the transience of beauty, the accidental pleasures
of travel, love and loss, the wisdom of age,
the unguarded tenderness of children,
religion and politics. Walking through these pages,
I wasn't "just reading a book, [I] really
was reading the world."

Angela Narciso Torres

Author of Blood Orange

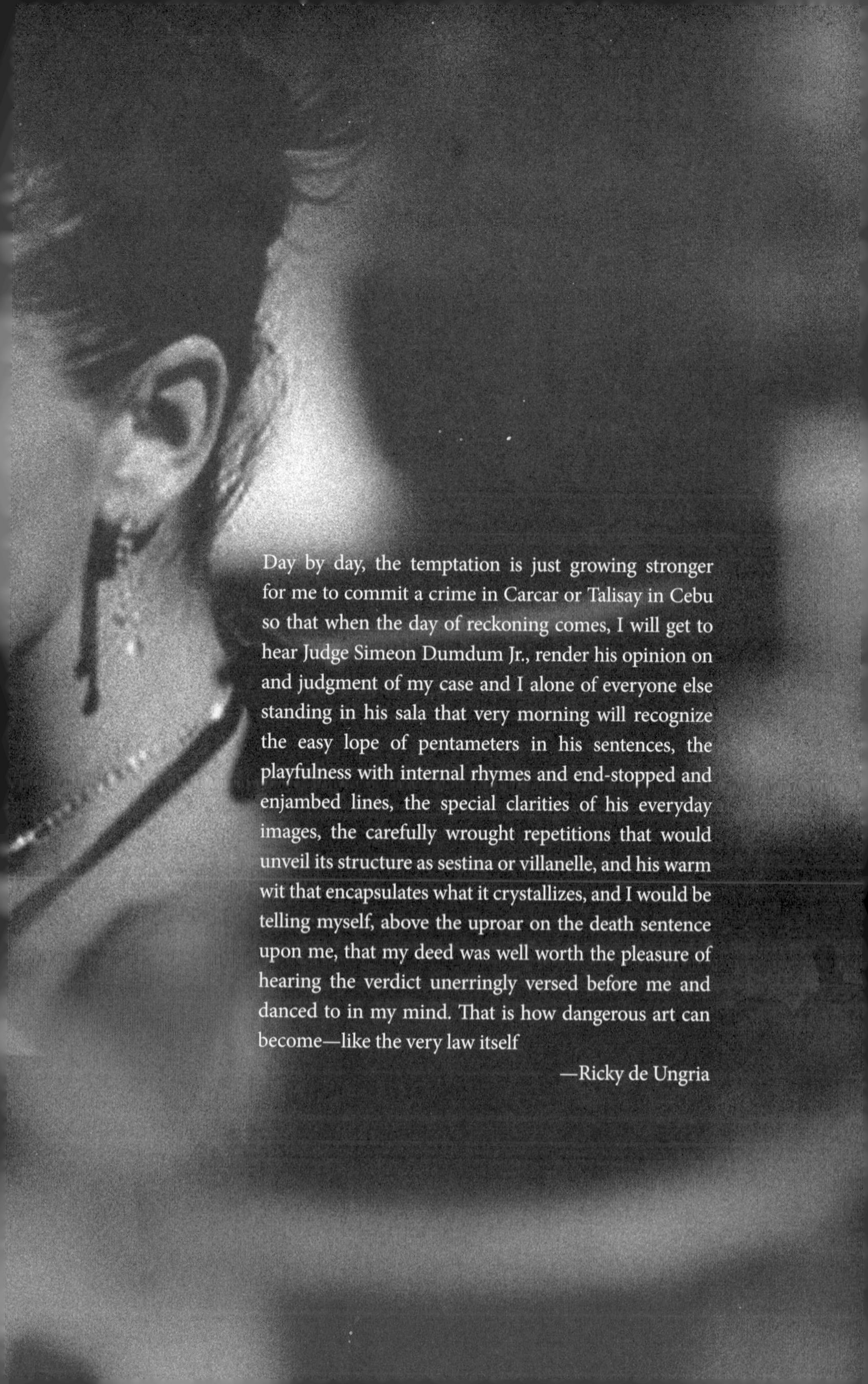

Day by day, the temptation is just growing stronger for me to commit a crime in Carcar or Talisay in Cebu so that when the day of reckoning comes, I will get to hear Judge Simeon Dumdum Jr., render his opinion on and judgment of my case and I alone of everyone else standing in his sala that very morning will recognize the easy lope of pentameters in his sentences, the playfulness with internal rhymes and end-stopped and enjambed lines, the special clarities of his everyday images, the carefully wrought repetitions that would unveil its structure as sestina or villanelle, and his warm wit that encapsulates what it crystallizes, and I would be telling myself, above the uproar on the death sentence upon me, that my deed was well worth the pleasure of hearing the verdict unerringly versed before me and danced to in my mind. That is how dangerous art can become—like the very law itself

—Ricky de Ungria

OTHER BOOKS BY THE AUTHOR

Poetry

The Gift of Sleep
Third World Opera
Poems Selected and New
If I Write You This Poem, Will You Make It Fly
To the Evening Star
Eighty-Four Words for Sorrow
Letter from Fatima
Partly Cloudy

Non-fiction

Love in the Time of the Camera
My Pledge of Love Cannot Be Broken
Ah, Wilderness

THE AUTHOR

Simeon Dumdum Jr. resides with his wife, Ma. Milagros, in Mohon, Talisay City, Cebu, Philippines. He once worked in the judiciary. His work—poems and non-fiction—has received several awards.

THE POET LEARNS TO DANCE

THE DANCER LEARNS TO WRITE A POEM

ACKNOWLEDGMENTS:
"Why It is Wrong to Cut Down Trees" appeared in
Prairie Schooner.

THE POET LEARNS TO DANCE

THE DANCER LEARNS TO WRITE A POEM

POEMS BY
SIMEON DUMDUM JR

BOOK DESIGN AND COVER ART BY
JOHANNA MICHELLE LIM

FOR GINGGING

CONTENTS

INTRODUCTION

I have two left feet. But this did not deter me from marrying a gazelle of a woman—in terms of grace not speed, because her endowments have not made her aerodynamic.

My wife dances well. During a tango, her toes touch the floor with the lightness of a Chinese brush on silk, her head and neck inclined like a lily. She knows my desire to trip the light fantastic and does not waste an opportunity to teach me the crossovers and chicken walks of Swing, for instance. Which effort only deepens my realization that birth has destined my feet for no more than country walks.

At one time, while watching my wife do the slow slow quick quick of the Foxtrot, I thought of Paul Valéry's "Poetry is to prose as dancing is to walking." I had just read Mary Oliver's "Rules for the Dance" and so found the circumstances conspiring to extract a confession from me, that I, an aspiring poet, likewise stood within the circle of dancers.

Dance has put its soul within rhythm, under an overlay of pattern and repetition. But it paces about like a caged animal. The passion arises from the dancer's having to merge into the moves the preoccupations of the heart and the resurgence of dreams deferred. Which only adds tension to the performance, because all the while, through inner ruses, ploys or schemes, they seek to break out and wreak havoc. For indeed the affective, the stream of thoughts and feelings, continues whether one dances or not, no matter what one does, even when one

sleeps and the riverbed of rationality turns into shifting sand. What can we do, the rules say that life should find freshness and power by conforming itself to the moves and the music and become a dance to the music of time. Chaos partners with meaning in a dance.

The same thing happens or should happen in a poem. One dances with the meaning and sound of words, which necessarily one must harness into a team. No matter how free the verse, the words must trot in tandem, like foxes that despite their wildness must keep to a clip-clop on the road of a morning in the country. A poem must dance. A poem must foxtrot or forever walk as prose.

JUSTICE ASPIRES TO THE CONDITION OF MUSIC

In court my gavel is authority
Whenever I bang it all noise ends
I sent two women out who talked too loudly
And warned a lawyer when his cellphone rang
If both the truth and the lie were a pin
Dropped in the courtroom, I would like to hear it
Its ting might be the small, still voice of justice
So just imagine my shock when one morning
While the accused was insisting that he
Was somewhere else on the night of the crime
From a tree outside came the trill of birdsong
So sweet that we all looked at where it came from
And the complainant felt set to forgive
And I, the useless gavel in my hand,
Yielded the moment to a better witness

A GHAZAL FOR MY FRIENDS AT CHRISTMAS

If Time can show me how, with felt-tip plow,
To write for you just now, a Christmas vow

To make the Christmas deep, and mountain-wide,
And with its words endow, a Christmas vow

For whatever it means, I think I know,
It's ever in my brow, a Christmas vow

And yet it's always you, yielding or set,
Who grant or disallow, a Christmas vow

Simeon, look at the sky, its script of rain
Is part of it somehow, a Christmas vow.

A LETTER TO PEDRO CALUNGSOD

Dear Pedro, that this letter will reach you
Is sure, unlike before—sailing in time,
The slow boats were overtaken by death
Or oblivion, how airheaded is love,
Which otherwise tells of a power that's greater
Than typhoons and thrusts of blade or spear.

And youthful hopes can be broached by a spear
Into a flood of grace—this we see in you.
Than money and power, is there nothing greater?
Must life be laid on the lap of time,
Untaught or neglectful of such as love,
Certain of nothing but the fact of death?

Adventure is of youth, but never death.
At your age, one went to sea with a spear—
To fish—but you went with Diego for love
Of the Word, finding life in Him, and you
Crossed the Pacific, to fish—for souls this time,
In Tumhon, a richer catch and a greater.

Youth counts in combat, nothing could be greater
Than quickness of mind and limb, because death,
They say, does not happen before it's time,
When the mundane hour hand becomes a spear.
But you did not let the heathen miss you
Again, for, set on its head, Death is Love.

How far from you the land of earthly love
For somehow you knew that there was a greater
Place that was calling for Diego and you,
Which Jesus had recompensed with his death,
Confirmed by the thrust of a soldier's spear—
A land that lies before and after time.

The Tumhon sea is as constant as time,
And the men shuttle between work and love,
And sleep, while their wives clean the fishing spear
For yet another day, nursing a greater
Dream, perhaps one that comes true beyond death,
And which someone welcomed, and this was you.

When you refused to duck a second time,
You showed us that, as between Death and Love,
Love is the greater, and the sharper spear.

LANDSCAPE ACCORDING TO CARAVAGGIO

They say that Caravaggio painted
As though he were inside a dungeon
Or a room deep within a tavern,
Where the illumination comes
Not from the sun but from a lamp,
Which is unseen and seems embedded
Into the very fact of being —
The women, children, men and horses,
Whose physicality is such
As to invite a curious finger,
Which makes his most reproduced painting,
"The Incredulity of St. Thomas,"
Somewhat a statement of his art.
Well then, what can we say of his
"Rest on the Flight into Egypt,"
In which he chose to yield himself
To do a sort of landscape painting,
Conceding to the sky a role?
That Biblical journey to Egypt
Offered for Caravaggio's use

The moment when Joseph decided —
After a glance at Mary and Child —
That it was time to take a breather.
I've come across the many legends
That grew out of this episode
And Caravaggio must have known
One or two stories of the kind —
For instance, how the Family
Found a spot in a grove of trees,
Which the Child ordered to bend down
And lay their fruit on Joseph's hand,
Their roots forthwith to yield a spring
For them to drink from and be filled.
Save for the trees, none of these stories
Finds telling in this lovely painting,
Lovely because of its resplendence,
No matter if a bit stylized —
A coiffured Mary and the Infant
Sleep with their heads touching each other,
An indication of how long
The journey so far travelled was,
And deep the dreams must be for them,
Speaking of which the wakeful Joseph,
Here shown as usual, an old man,
Has never run out of — in dreams

God spoke to him, and through an angel,
Such as the one that we see here —
Young, winged, draped in linen,
Which functions but as a fig leaf —
And this, the presence of the angel,
Playing a vintage violin
As Joseph holds up before him
Sheet music from the Song of Songs,
Hints at this being a dream, too,
Or an interpretation of
Something that has already happened,
Which, whether old or new, all art,
If it be true, is all about,
And in this work of Caravaggio's
All else is past — except the sky,
Odd for someone like Caravaggio,
An artist who made use of darkness,
Which here he had at last to part
To show a glow out of the gloom,
A sky that came to light towards
The morning of the Resurrection.

A LOVE POEM

If a lover, eye a suitor, fool every star
Tell any aster dye, tie all in a yesterday
We like to gather, walk together
Aha old am I you hound hold my hand
I'll ease as on I go all is song
What words whet we our odes
One does live here and so I love her
Look, no lie dies young, like an old saying

TANKA

Every little rose
Lifted up by a finger
Like a lover's chin
Looks at you with its dewdrops
And desires to be a ring

ART HISTORY
(FOR JARED SEBASTIAN)

Until I saw a satellite view
Of the earth, and the line separating
Day from night, which moved as the earth turned,
I never really understood
Caravaggio.

Until I caught in Caravaggio
The conversation between light
And darkness, and the wisdom,
Which only silence could impart,
I never really understood
The meaning of story.

Until I told a little boy
A curious tale, and he was afraid
And ran outside the room, and then,
When I had lost hope that he would
Return, and I could end my story,
I heard his steps and saw him stand

Within the shadow of the door,
I never fully understood
The meaning of love.

AT THE BOAT TERMINAL

We arrived two hours before boarding
Our boat was still returning from Ormoc
The wife and I looked for good seats
Where we could spend the waiting time
And I sat basking in her presence
Whose warmth induced a somnolence
I drifted in and out of sleep
And every time that I awakened
The sight that met me was a door
Which had a framed view of the ocean
And was my hold on wakefulness
I saw another waiting fastcraft
Lying along one of the piers
Noting its gentle rise and fall
I thought it seemed a brooch that clasped
The bosom of a breathing sea

AT THE LOBBY OF THE CASINO ESPAÑOL DE CEBU

The water drips from every side
Of each of three reddish-brown basins,
The smaller higher than the bigger,
The last spilling into a pond
Breathing with multi-colored carp.
The scene speaks of something beyond me—
Eternity? If so, there is
No better place to wait for you,
Whose entrance is indefinite.
I mark my wait with the unhurried
Fall of water from the fountain,
Continuous like that of light
Endlessly writing on the pond
A script I will never decipher,
Which no fish will bother to read
Because already they understand.

BESIDE THE SEA

If this moan is a soft hiss of the sameness of the sea
Time looks up from the tide pool at me, like a spoof, a room
that outed a plea
Sail on again, hero, daub a fire so long unheard before
Caress a soul if he lunges here across a self-healing shore
If ending is a lie, pat a hoarse doe finding sleep at her side
It's time to hear a sung étude to stem the rising tide

CUP

Gently I cradled the cup with my hands
(How like a baby the tap water slept),
I must take care the water would not spill.
That the measure had to be right was crucial
(Said the book, lying on the other side
Of the room, next to the fruit and the blender).
Beginner that I was, I should take pains—
To lose a drop would be to lose it all.
And as I walked under the ceiling lamp,
I saw its image mirrored on the water.
When held a little to the side, the cup
Echoed a portion of the living room,
The wall on which hung the family portrait—
It seemed the morning light was teaching me
A way of looking, and that I would see
The whole of the interior of the house
If I raised the cup and moved it about,
As if in benediction.

GOSSAMER

Today the morning is as clear as glass.
It seems it has been this way where I live—
Unbroken resplendence even in furtive
Things, and the frail and elusive show class.
Light gropes the shade that hides behind the mass
Of leaves, and there is nothing fugitive
To wakeful eyes now, nothing elusive,
Everything glows with the dew on the grass,
And none more than the splayed web of a spider
That has tied itself to a pliant sapling
In the sun's path—it is as though a bullet
Was fired right into the sun's fiery river,
Leaving a spider of a hole, and cracking
The glass of morning without breaking it.

IN A SMALL CAFÉ

I tell myself, it all may see life,
This marigold, ethos more ogled
Than sunrise, thin as one rose,
Far in eye or eaves, afire on your vase,
On a fat rune neon coif one afternoon in a café
Ah roar were aids, here are words
Crossing, caressing
Here to see flow a rathe to agree, a wise heart is a flower that grows
Out ahead voice fugue trees—the advice of guitars
Live by need, toil along, love beyond telling

LOVE AT THE MALL

His left hand clutched a droopy shopping bag
While his right jealously guarded her hips
And I had nothing to say to myself
I really just happened to follow them
After the rain pushed me inside the mall
I was sure, though I could not see their faces,
That the light of the morning moved with them
And became almost eternal because
At times they stopped and hardly ever stirred
Not even when a little orange ball
Rolled from the games department on my right
Towards the feet of the love-leaning girl
Who merely flicked the stray thing with her heels,
And then it just rolled back to where it came
I never saw a more obedient ball

OHOY BUTTERFLY WINGS

La la la la la

Ohoy butterfly wings, if you fly do it today
The sun sets and the clock may not tell more than the time
The next day that arrives will again start to depart
As he takes her hand in the garden of the roses

La la la la la

Ohoy butterfly wings, when you're gone it will be night
The cold winds are now blowing, the brown leaves start to fall
And words fail to remind as they float weightless as fluff
The sea in the distance recedes as far as nothing

La la la la la

Ohoy butterfly wings, from my study I can glimpse
The green world and your flicker of pride over the flowers
These two wings could be mine as I write day after day
They close like a life on a shelf with light as bookends

La la la la la

SARABANDE

Look at the violin player, notice her hand
Slither along the slender fingerboard
And how she swings the bow—a gossamer sword
That wounds the strings into a sarabande,
Slow as the tide receding from the strand,
And then three strings call loudly as a chord,
Sudden, as though at last the soul was gored,
And they who witnessed it were moved to stand.
And now the dance begins, as if on tiptoe
The couple step lightly just as before
When they had love and had no fear of losing,
And as the sea wills what things come and go,
Gently their every foot writes on the floor
About a door opening and then closing.

SPRINGTIME IN JAPAN

There was no petal of the cherry blossom
Which we had asked of her, since it was spring
Near Osaka—instead, she chose to bring
A story, which she recounted through the prism
Of old Japan, and the timeless truism
Of woman's virtue, of which they still sing
In the Kabuki, but the art in the floating
World of Hokusai appears somewhat gruesome,
For there Okiku, who was forced to run
And jump into a well to put a stop
To her master's advances, would appear
As ghost, which I doubt, but I feel that when
One draws water from the well, the first drop
Spilling out of the pail may be a tear.

ST. FRANCIS AND THE HOUSE OF STONE AND MORTAR

Francis came back to Mary of the Angels
And was aghast to see an awful sight—
A prodigious house made of stone and mortar,
Which meant that everything that Francis said
Concerning poverty the brethren scorned,
That their huts be made of wattle and daub
And show but a pitiable design.
He found the worldly seeming of the house too much
And so, bidding his brethren to join him,
He got astride the roof and ripped a tile,
Having in mind to tear the whole house down.
He would have kept at it but for the soldiers,
Who told him that the house did not belong
To them but to the people of Assisi.
How much this speaks of the writing of poems,
Which often starts with abject poverty,
A stripping down to being's very core,
Where suddenly I find Beauty itself
And claim it as my own, this loveliness,
This gift that I must not touch with my doubts.

THE POET LEARNS TO DANCE (THE DANCER LEARNS TO WRITE A POEM)

Let your hand rest like a bird on my left hip
Let your mind rest where it is cool and quiet
With your left, hold my right hand at this height
With your lips let the words roll out and skip
So move your foot with mine for just a snip
So catch that word flying away—it's right
Relax, your hold on me should not be tight
Relax, the images have their own script
Now turn as if to accept and decline
Now use a rhyme and do your best to keep it
At times the swaying makes you feel bourgeois
At times words send a tingle down your spine
It looks as if I am writing a sonnet
It feels as if I am dancing the Cha-cha

WHY I JUST LEFT THE SEA ALONE

In fact I had a camera.
I felt the need to carry one
Because we were guests at a wedding,
At which no move can be a move
Unless attended by the click
Of an intrusive camera.
But weddings have an undercurrent
That's undeterred by the stock flotsam
That marks our every ceremony,
And this I saw in a child's tugging
At the maroon gown of her mother,
Which I thought meant that it was time
For her—and bride and groom—to go,
Across whichever blue her mind
Conceived the journey, which for her
Was marked from playtime to playtime,
And in the end amounted to home.
Ambushed by aimless conversation,
The wife and I prepared to leave
When wine and guests began to ebb.

As we walked, passing by a window,
I saw the sea, but I just stared,
Finding the waves too slow, either
For camera or memory.

WHY I LEAVE FOOTPRINTS

They are gone, the shoes
I should have bought yesterday
Tears flow from my feet

WHY THE FAN HAS A MIND OF ITS OWN

A carpet was unrolled, then strewn
With petals, mostly of red roses,
On which the couple were to walk
When word was given by the planner,
Now endlessly fanning herself
As she attended to the details
(With its red and white rays, the fan
Fluttered like a mad butterfly
Lamenting the disarrayed petals,
Which really were thrown there on purpose.)
Now that all loose ends had been tied up,
She gave the signal, and the couple
Marched in accordance with her music
And pre-rehearsed choreography.
But suddenly, while everyone
Was clapping in lusty approval,
They kissed before reaching the altar—
He wrapped his arms around her back
And swung her upwards in the air,
Her feet curved up into a U—

The bell of a saxophone, which
He had to bend backwards to blow.
Which kiss transfixed the rest of us
And stopped us dead in our tracks,
And nothing moved—except the fan.

WINDOW

My wish is to see the small window open
To let the gaze reach as far as it goes
And make a wider and bigger view happen

The roses climb upwards as if to sharpen
Whatever picture they might want to compose
To grant my wish to see the window open

And I who stand below feel so misshapen
Because of an insistent breeze that blows
To make a wider and bigger view happen

Did I just see the flicker of a hairpin?
Again the morning is too full of glows
For me not to wish that the window would open

And let such story that I think of deepen
As the small window chooses to disclose
To make a wider and bigger view happen

Perhaps to throw it out into a half spin,
A hand might reach out for the topmost rose—
For my wish to see the small window open
And make a wider and bigger view happen

WHY IT IS WRONG TO CUT DOWN TREES

The chickens were back
As if nothing had happened,
As if the land of their roost,
A guava tree,
Had not been sold,
And the owner of the land
Had not fled the country,
Tired of having always
To start his business
After every coup attempt,
And hearing, whenever
His sales would pick up,
Of mysterious troop movements
In the capital.
They were again in the yard,
As if the new owner,
An old colonel,
Whose estate far exceeded his pay
And who had hoped for a position
In the supposed junta,

Had not cut down
The guava tree
In his frustration at the failure
Of the rebel soldiers.
The chickens,
Which had grown in number
From the union
Of a leaf-brown hen and a phantom cock,
Which started to roost in the tree
As five siblings,
Occupying first the lowest five branches,
And had multiplied
(Because the phantom kept reappearing)
To fill up all the branches,
Still returned to roost,
Taking the same places
As they had done from the start,
As if the tree were still there,
So that now they stood
On top of each other,
And the mad colonel
Further lost his mind
When—out of habit formed
In the field as soldier—
He broke his sleep
To relieve himself outdoors
And in the moonlight saw the ghost
Of the guava tree.

FLORENCE

Is history a way of walking?
Our eager guide seemed to agree
And before sunset she made us
Walk up and down the streets of Florence.
First, we paraded—all of us—
To Santa Maria del Fiore,
And gazed at Giotto's Campanille,
The Baptistry with its bronze doors
And, as we walked away, the Duomo.
Our feet were like dumb beasts of burden
Carrying us from street to street.
At Piazza Della Signoria
We had an instant photograph
With Michaelangelo's David,
At Chiesa di Ognisanti,
Glimpsing at Giotto's Crucifix,
I read from Second Timothy
During a Mass arranged for us
By a grey-garbed nun from Cebu.
And then we had pasta and wine

At a trattoria near the Arno.
As we passed Dante's monument
At Piazza di Santa Croce
I asked myself if poetry
Were not as well a walking thing,
And echoing him I cried, "Poet,
By that God to you unknown,
Lead me this way." (Saying, "Follow,"
The ancient cabinet that night
In our hotel knocked as I paced
The floor, and for a while I thought
That someone was walking with me.)

PISA

As we lined up for the ride that would take us
To near the Piazza dei Miracoli
Where we would see them all—the Cathedral,
The Baptistery and, of course, the Bell Tower—
A hawker of umbrellas poked my ribs
When I refused to buy one of his articles,
And made my entry into the bus faster.
After we got down, we walked a short distance
Past shops that sold various souvenir items,
And there it was, the Leaning Tower, exactly
As it appeared in photographs and books,
And the heart felt a fullness at the sight
Of an imagined thing right before it,
And yet we came because of an illusion,
To which a little dog a lady pulled
Across the edge of the lawn of the piazza
Seemed to agree—it looked at the Bell Tower,
And must have wondered that there should exist,
Between man's vertical reality
And the flat horizontal world of dogs,
The charming half-truth of the Leaning Tower.

ASSISI

We could not leave St. Mary of the Angels
Without a group photograph at the patio,
And then it would be night in a few hours.
The wife and I came out of the museum,
Wended our way past a well in the courtyard,
Hearing, as we walked, the monks chanting Vespers.
Everyone else had left except ourselves.
Missing something, I thought of going back
Inside the basilica to spend time,
Alone and undisturbed, in the small church,
The "Little Portion" or Porziuncola,
And there become one with the ancient bricks
That flickered with the candle flame when Francis
Cut off Clare's hair, changed her velvet clothes
With a coarse gown, and capped her with a veil,
Or else, behind the big basilica,
In the Rose Garden, the water that gushed
Out of the tilted well at the same time
That Francis rolled like a wheel on the brambles
To conquer doubts and the lures of the flesh

(The brambles turned into thornless dog roses).
I wanted to be intimate with them—
Eyewitnesses of the ineffable,
And I may not be able to return,
Our one-way pilgrimage was almost done,
And our guide, flag in hand, was calling us
To gather for a group picture before we walked
To the bus that would take us to Spoleto,
And as we smiled for the photographer,
There rose above St. Mary of the Angels
The same round moon that Francis called his sister.

VIDEO NIGHT IN SPOLETO

Spoleto was our refuge for a night
So cold that we shivered, we and the stars,
But there of course it was just yesterlight,
Vision of memory, unlike in Mars,
Unpulsing as a heart which had no scars,
Unlike my own, which journeyed for forgiveness
And struggled with night's doubts and faithlessness

AVILA

Teresa, here we are, clothed with the mist
Of Autumn, which is kind in Avila.
At once the wife takes a shot of the door,
The same door that, when only twenty one,
You entered, thence devoting a full thirty
Of your inspirited sixty seven years
At the Monasterio de la Encarnación.
The courtyard has a path towards a cross,
A set of seven steps serially numbered—
The seven mansions that you wrote about
In the "Interior Castle"—which I take,
A quick, vicarious journey of the soul,
This before our guide Maria hurries us
Through the three parlors, then up the stairs
To the museum with its lit glass cases,
but I stop, seeing an unusual statue,
Clad in a robe of black and purple stripes,
That of St. Joseph, which, they say, you put
To spy upon the nuns while you were out,
Which explains why the statue has large ears.
I look at it and contemplate the humor

That poetry and sanctity must have
To be astonishing—your Ecstasy,
For instance (hard to believe that it happened
Among the furniture of a small chapel
Inside this convent), when a small. bright angel
Thrust into your heart a long, golden spear,
Fire-tipped, that made you moan with a sweet pain.
Who says that God's love is not physical?
Incorrupt years after your death, your heart
Displayed inexplicable punctures.
Again your account of this event carries
A hint of your characteristic jesting:
"If anyone thinks that I am lying,
I pray the Lord, in His infinite goodness,
To give to him the very same experience"—
And yet I'll take your word for it, Teresa,
I will give you my doubt at anytime
As barter for a perforated heart.

SANTAREM, PORTUGAL

In Santarem, October's tide
Of yellow leaves was here and there,
There was a bench which I ascended,
The better to take photographs
Of the church patio's olive trees.
The while, a woman dressed in red
Gazed at me from an upper window
Opening out of a brick wall.
It must have been a common sight—
Foreigners visiting the Church
Of the Most Holy Miracle—
And now this group of bundled Asians.
Time can bleed one's faith of freshness,
And the account of how the curtain
Was drawn away from human eyes
To show God's presence in the bread—
Fated to be told constantly
To every wide-eyed visitor—
Must have become as much a chore
As any other in the home.
If she, the woman at the window,

Happened to have this disposition
I'd understand, and hoped that she
Would likewise understand that I
Would come to Portugal, and even
Stand on the cleft of any rock
Just so I could see the Lord's back
As Moses when God's glory passed,
Which was why I was in Santarem,
Having climbed behind the tabernacle
To view the consecrated host—
The blood had settled in the pyx
For more than seven hundred years
After the priest retrieved the host
Which bled in the hands of a wife
About to give it to a witch
To use as potion to reverse
Her husband's infidelity.
What world did the woman see daily
From her upstairs window, stretching
As far as the River Tagus?
What world was it that I saw flowing
From the glass tabernacle window,
As though an endless river streaming
Through a sudden gap in the rocks?

SALAMANCA

A cold wind blew when we arrived.
The rain that fell in Portugal
Followed us like a batty dog.
But in Salamanca the sun,
Flying to somewhere beyond Spain,
Joined us at the Plaza Mayor,
Where we got off for a brief visit.
We had time just for the cathedral
And briskly we walked towards it
As to an only relative
In a strange city, less an act
Of obligation, however,
Than an attempt to validate
Our presence here, but the cathedral
Was closed, so we took photographs
Of just the doors and marigolds
Still in bloom, though it was late autumn,
Whose frosts might have missed the
front garden,
On purpose, I hasten to add,
This being Salamanca—to which

Victor, a chance acquaintance, who
By way of aiding our memory
Mentioned Victor Hugo,
Would agree, as he talked about
The city of his affections
Over a cup of cappuccino.
He glorified a copy of
A Dello Delli table, one
Of those displayed in the cathedral,
"The Adoration of the Magi,"
The wife had purchased on impulse
From the university store,
But I would have chosen a poster
That said, "Quod natura non dat,
Salmantica non praestat."
Outside, a man walked with his dog,
Without delay a cop arrived
And said something to the dog owner.
There was the chilly wind again.
Time to return to the old bus,
Thinking of Victor's parting shot,
"There's no Salamanca without
The university and tourists."
Tourists? So part of Salamanca
Are those that are just passing through—
The sun, the wind, the rain—and me.

NOTRE DAME CATHEDRAL, PARIS

I must be blank to make all this adhere
To my footloose and easygoing soul,
Disguised as a tourist out for a stroll.
Nothing will stay of what I see and hear,
And not just the Galerie des Chimères.
Unless I keep still, each pane or gargoyle
Will just pass through a tear in time, a hole
In memory, and then will disappear.
The stories told are of infinity,
The reason why the stained glass lights are singing
An oratorio as a choir of rainbows.
Without this emptying, I would just be
A totally tattooed man contemplating
The uses of the north and south rose windows.

RAIN IN BANGKOK

It rains this morning in Bangkok.
From our hotel room I can see
The National Stadium in the haze,
And far off like a Hershey kiss
A temple, gold behind the veil
Of Bangkok's early morning drizzle.
This is our second day, tomorrow
Is our Chao Phraya River cruise,
Which seems for us a sort of duty,
Being first-timers in Thailand.
Oh it's not that I'm complaining.
With you beside me, every sight
Is a virtual Temple of Dawn
And every walk a river cruise
Beside another urban river,
The rolling BTS Skytrain,
Which even now is rumbling by
For Chit Lom, heading towards Bearing.
Most things seem to be flowing here,
For where, I really do not know.
We're hand in hand—if I got lost

You'd be a blind train in a storm
Though I was only in the lobby.
Back and forth you would pass by me,
Face covered by the Bangkok Post.

EARTHQUAKE

Always it starts with a tiny sound,
No louder than the clink of ice in a glass—
The little Venus on the table
Tick-tocks as it walks in a wobble,
The frame beside it slowly slides,
The books begin to leave the shelves
As though pulled out by many readers,
And the vase, after a tap dance,
Leans on a side and topples over,
Its water like a hand of tears
Trying to retrieve the spilled roses,
And then the falling starts in earnest—
The miniature Venus de Milo
Drops to the floor to join its arms
In the unseen world of the broken,
The portraits kiss the floor and break,
Glasses and plates, all things untied,
Fall out and shatter on the tiles,
And those that are attached swing wildly,
The cuckoo comes out of its closet
To shout an anonymous hour,

As the whole house itself convulses
With the now fast unsettling ground.

Terror comes at a given morning
Which otherwise we might forget,
Expecting mornings to be the usual—
Sunny and with a hint of breeze,
Quiet but for the kindly tinkle
Of teaspoon in a coffee cup—
And yet it is that kind of morning
When suddenly disaster strikes
And it could be the end of time—
We rush out of the creaking house
And hold each other as the ground
Heaves and churns, threatening to open
And swallow up what is above it,
Our prayers get louder, they're almost
Like shouts, we want them physically
To lift us from the angry ground,
A neighbor's house smokes at the sides
Which twisting has turned into powder,
"Lord, save us!" we cry, "Mary help us!"

Before we know it, it is over,
That is the way with such as earthquakes,
That's what they share with a fine day,
So passing it is, like a sunset,
And then it's dark, we hope to hear
Again the voices of our children
And in our arms to gather them,
Enclose them with a wall of sobs.

In time we hear of other cries
Louder than ours, of other places
That were spun faster and bounced higher
By the unspeakable upheaval,
Perhaps the people there were like us,
Having just risen from their sleep,
Or else in church for early Mass,
We only hear of news about them
And, of course, see the photographs—
Roads with cracks so huge they go down
To the earth's dark, mysterious heart,
The splintered bridges hanging limply
Like the strips of a burst balloon,
And over where once stood the homes
And the enormous ancient churches
The dust hangs, staying behind like a parent
In the place where a child was lost.

What I find strange is that the statue
Of Mary the Mother of God
Is often all that has remained,
Intact but for a nick or two,
Among the heartbreaking debris.
But about faith and its mystery,
After my heart has trembled with the earth,
Nothing now comes as a surprise—
Is that not where you should stand, Mary,
Wherever there is devastation,
Just as you stood under the Cross?

BALLADE: INSTRUCTIONS TO AN AID WORKER

You're on the ground dropped from the sky
Your parachute laden with food,
Water, and medicines in dry
Parcels—you have no time to brood
And whatever may be your mood
You have to meld your mind and heart.
Begin your task, do not be rude
Empty yourself and then depart

Now you must be hearing their cry
The wind and waves have stripped them nude
There is a tear in every eye
But things are worse than what you've viewed
And redder than the blood they spewed
Hit by the walls falling apart
Just do your work and then conclude
Empty yourself and then depart

I know that you might wish to die
Seeing the lifeless children blued
By hours, but there's no time to buy

Already, the people have chewed
Everything but food, and the shrewd
Have ransacked stores and homes to cart
Away anything they find good
Empty yourself and then depart

You move around, do not be glued
By your emotions, aid is art—
That which you seek cannot elude
Empty yourself and then depart

A LIGHT SHINES AT THE BOTTOM OF NOTHING

The little girl jostled with everyone
For noodles, rice, water and groceries—
Whatever food might go into the packs
Piled up inside the military van.
The typhoon struck the dawn with a whiplash
And then like many evil hands the waves
Pulled out her father, mother and two brothers
Fast beyond all crying and reaching out,
For days she had been roaming without food
When by chance she saw the van and rushed to it,
Save that it seemed that the whole world did too—
With faster, longer, stronger legs and arms.
God knows she did her best, her lungs were bursting,
But everybody got inside the van
Ahead of her, and she just bit her finger
While she watched the men and women and the boys
Cradle their load as though it were a loot
And quickly disappear into the dark.
Still she went up to gather what was left
And in the van her foot felt a round thing,
A flashlight, all that remained of the pile,

Which she picked up and used on her way out,
Back to her usual corner near a wall,
And when she shook from the cold and the hunger,
She put the glaring flashlight in her mouth
And radiant as oranges her cheeks glowed—
Night had not seen a more magical lantern.

WHAT REMAINS OF THE SKY

After a typhoon
That snipped the roof of our house
We huddle at night
Awake in each other's arms—
Hey, is that the moon or what?

THE TEST OF FRIENDSHIP

In this park by the sea
is a series of lamp posts,
each with two heads,
on which pigeons would alight
in equal numbers.
A typhoon came
and cut off some of the posts.
The pigeons still alight
on the street lamps
but only on those still with heads.
Those they have shunned,
the decapitated ones,
now know
that true friendship
is not always
a matter of wings.

AFTER THE STORM

The brown shrike's call announced that the typhoon
Already was a day's journey away
And was so far from us any delay
Would not cost us a lovely afternoon.
The bird was at the height of a balloon,
Near the eaves, where it decided to stay
And be safe, out of the savage wind's way,
In which trees, roofs and walls were ripped and strewn.
How could I not find in it a suggestion
That what is indestructible is feather
Not stone, whatever is as light as spirit,
Which, as I cleaned the yard, called my attention
To its companionship, this other creature
The storm had missed—joy it must sing to share it.

THAN TREES

Love we may call what is greater than trees
Because it rises much taller than trees

They sit before a little waterfall
And they to me appear bigger than trees

I'm on a bridge standing across from them
They see nothing of me other than trees

Because love does strange things to gravity
They must be flying now higher than trees

Because what grows has a voice of its own
But love can be so much louder than trees

Because their love will last beyond their time
The mortal lovers live longer than trees

But then most things end with the afternoon
Whose light has brought the dark closer than trees

They walk towards me who must move away
And find another place farther than trees

Because your love now bids me come home, calling,
"Simeon," and to me you're dearer than trees.